SCAR
WARS

ISBN: 978-1-63308-623-4 Paperback
         978-1-63308-624-1 Digital

Interior and Cover Design by R'tor John D. Maghuyop

CHALFANT ECKERT
PUBLISHING

1028 S Bishop Avenue, Dept. 178
Rolla, MO 65401

Printed in United States of America

SCAR WARS

DR. RON WEBB

Author of *Leadership From Behind the Scenes*

CHALFANT ECKERT

PUBLISHING

TABLE OF CONTENTS

CHAPTER 1

EVERYONE HAS A SCAR STORY

But he was wounded for our transgressions,
he was bruised for our iniquities:
the chastisement of our peace was upon him;
and with his stripes we are healed.

Isaiah 53:5

Scars remind us of earlier wounds that healed but left living testimonies of circumstances and events that we endured and survived. Jesus has the most impactful scar story of all ages. He who knew no sin endured chastisement, mockery, unwarranted judgment, physical pain, and death on the Cross for our sins. He endured the Cross and survived the shame, humiliation, and unfair treatment and now sits at the right hand of God the Father making intercession for you and me. He knows what we are going through, and He knows how our scars can influence and shape our lives and futures.

Some scars are physical, some mental, some emotional, and some spiritual. Some are temporary and short-lived; others are permanent and stay with us for life. A scar forms where a wound used to be. Physical scars are visible and often have a story behind them. You can point to a physical scar and recall the story of how you got it and share it with others. That is seldom true of mental, emotional, and spiritual scars. They are not as easily recognized and are often hidden and never shared for fear of being judged or ridiculed, or because you are afraid the pain of the original wound will be brought back to the surface and you will have to live through it again. Even when others cannot see our scars, we all have them and they all tell a story.

I am going to share some of my scar stories with you in this book, and I encourage you to share your scar stories with others. From the sharing, we come to understand that we are not alone – many people share the same scars. They may be hidden in different places, but stem from the same kinds of wounds. When we open up and share with others, we stop focusing on ourselves and get about the Father's work in the Kingdom. God put us here to be salt and light, and when we shine a light on our hidden scars, we encourage others to go on in their pain because they can see in us that wounds heal and life goes on, even if scars are left from the experience. We would not be the first to share our hidden pain so that others could benefit. Heaven is filled with a cloud of witnesses looking down from the balconies encouraging us with their scar stories. Here are just a few examples of the scar stories that continue to give Christians hope year after year because instead of hiding their grief, pain, and scars, these people shared their scars and turned them into great hymns of the faith that have brought comfort to millions ever since:

1. Horatio Spafford was a Chicago lawyer who lost all his properties in a fire in 1871. A few years later, he sent his wife and daughters on a voyage that ended with the ship sinking, and all four of his daughters were drowned. In spite of the tragedies he lived through, he still had hope when he wrote *It Is Well With My Soul* in 1873. Can you hear the hope in his words? Can you feel the peace of his scars?

    When peace, like a river, attendeth my way,
    When sorrows like sea billows roll;
    Whatever my lot, Thou hast taught me to say,
    It is well, it is well with my soul.

    (These lyrics are in the Public Domain)

2. Louisa Stead watched from the shore as her husband tried to save a young boy from drowning. Both the husband and the boy

drowned. In 1882, there were no food stamps, no social security, and no help for widows with children. Amid their grief, Louisa and her daughter Lily came to the brink of starvation, destitute with no way to get food. But God knew the circumstances and miraculously provided them with food at just the right moment. Louisa sat down that night and penned the words to *'Tis So Sweet to Trust in Jesus*. Christians have hummed and sung that song for almost 140 years, and from her scars, many people have received God's comfort and reassurance of His promise to never leave or forsake them in time of trouble.

> *Tis so sweet to trust in Jesus,*
> *Just to take Him at His Word;*
> *Just to rest upon His promise,*
> *And to know, "Thus saith the Lord!"*

(These lyrics are in the Public Domain)

Shortly after writing this song, Louisa and Lily became missionaries to South Africa. From the ashes of their grief, God used their scars for the Kingdom.

3. Fanny Crosby got sick at six weeks old and as a result of treatment, lost her sight. She was poor and lived in a slum in New York. Her father died when she was six months old, and she was raised by her mother and grandmother. She attended a school for the blind where she learned to play several instruments and memorize whole books of the Bible including the Gospels. Later, she married a man who was also blind. They had a daughter who died shortly after birth, some say of typhoid fever. Her husband became a recluse, but Fanny kept writing hymns. She wrote over 8,000 hymns, many under pseudonyms because hymnal publishers did not feel comfortable having so many hymns written by the same person in one hymnal. She shared her scars and brought them out in ways that inspired others then and now. One of her most loved hymns was *Blessed Assurance*:

Blessed assurance, Jesus is mine!
O what a foretaste of glory divine!
Heir of salvation, purchase of God,
Born of His Spirit, washed in His blood.

Refrain:

This is my story, this is my song,
praising my Savior all the day long;
this is my story, this is my song,
praising my Savior all the day long.

Perfect submission, perfect delight!
Visions of rapture now burst on my sight;
Angels descending bring from above
Echoes of mercy, whispers of love.

Perfect submission, all is at rest!
I in my Savior am happy and blessed,
Watching and waiting, looking above,
Filled with His goodness, lost in His love.

(These lyrics are in the Public Domain)

Fanny once said that the first thing she wanted to *see* when she got to heaven was her Savior. She didn't let being blind stop her from positively influencing others. She poured her heart into sharing the hope behind the scars she carried.

I could give example after example of scarred people who turned scars from their misfortunes, tragic events, and deeply painful losses into blessings for others, but the most powerful scar story of all time comes from our Lord Jesus Christ. The Cross of Calvary has messy scars that serve as reminders to us that Jesus was fully divine and of the Godhead, but also fully human in flesh and blood. He felt deep pain, rejection, suffering, abandonment, ridicule, and humiliation. Isaiah tells us that Jesus was marred more than any man. What does that mean? The scars must have been horrendous. He was tortured with a cat o' nine tails containing pieces of metal, knots, perhaps glass and bones, or other instruments to tear skin. In the days of Roman scourging, it was also customary to throw salt in the wounds. The Bible doesn't tell us exactly how many lashes Jesus was given, but the customary number was thirty-nine lashes because that is what Jewish law called for. Thirty-nine lashes times nine pieces of braided leather imbedded with instruments to tear flesh would be 351 stripes. However, the lashes were given by the Romans, who were not under Jewish law, so no telling how many lashes Jesus had to endure. But to be marred more than any man, we know it was gruesome and horrific. Then after all that pain, He was nailed to a wooden Cross to die an agonizing death.

When Jesus appeared to his disciples, He wasn't in pain anymore. He was at peace. But He still had the holes in His hands and feet, a testimony to His suffering. His glorified body showed the disciples that there was hope for eternal life even with the scars.

If Jesus was willing to show His scars for the edification and comfort and hope of others, and we are supposed to be like Jesus, why are we afraid to show our wounds and scars? Oh, brothers and sisters, if we had more people willing to show their scars, we could bring healing to others who are hurting and without hope.

> *And they overcame him by the blood of the Lamb,*
> *and by the word of their testimony;*
> *and they loved not their lives unto the death.*
>
> Revelation 12:11

Your wounds and your scars are a part of your testimony. God knew that when He raised Jesus from the dead but did not heal His nail-scarred hands. He healed others but had scars. We have scars in common with our Savior and with other Christians.

What is keeping you from positively influencing others by sharing your scars? Your testimony could give comfort, bring peace, and let others know they are not alone. You don't have to be a hymn writer, evangelist, or preacher. You just need to be willing to let God use your scars to touch lives. Stop hiding the events that made you who you are and get moving! Refuse to give up, give in, or give out.

CHAPTER 2

SCARS OF LONELINESS

A man that hath friends must shew himself friendly:
and there is a friend that sticketh closer than a brother.

Proverbs 18:24

Loneliness affects millions of people daily, so much so that numerous studies have been done with surprising findings. One study indicated, "Lacking social connection carries a risk that is comparable, and in many cases, exceeds that of other well-accepted risk factors, including smoking up to 15 cigarettes per day, obesity, physical inactivity, and air pollution" (Holt-Lunstad et al., 2010). Loneliness increases with age, and some people feel lonely even when married. It is an emotional state that can lead to depression, sleeplessness, poor self-esteem, and even dementia. It can affect your mental health and lead to premature death. Loneliness comes in many forms and stems from many causes that produce wounds, pain, and scars.

If you are lonely, you are not alone! Many people in the Bible experienced loneliness including the Lord Jesus Christ. Isaiah 53:3 tells us:

He is despised and rejected of men; a man of sorrows,
and acquainted with grief: and we hid
as it were our faces from him;
he was despised, and we esteemed him not.

Can you imagine what it must have been like for Jesus? His brothers didn't believe him. He was asked to leave the Gadarenes. The Pharisees couldn't stand Him, and they plotted against Him. His disciples ran away when He was taken into custody. Judas betrayed Him. Peter denied Him three times. His closest friends wouldn't stay awake for even one hour to pray with Him. He was mocked, humiliated, beaten, and hung between thieves. And lastly, he felt separated from the Father and alone on the Cross.

And about the ninth hour Jesus cried
with a loud voice, saying,
Eli, Eli, lama sabachthani? that is to say,
My God, my God, why hast thou forsaken me?

Matthew 27:46

There could be a whole teaching series on Matthew 27 and Psalm 22, but for now, it is sufficient to say that even Jesus Christ felt the bitter sting of loneliness.

John experienced loneliness when he was sent to the Island of Patmos in AD 95 by the Roman Emperor Domitian for his "criminal" views on Christianity. It was an isolated volcanic island with almost no trees off the coast of what is now Turkey. Instead of going stir crazy, God gave him a mission, so John wrote to the seven churches of Asia.

Elijah called down fire from heaven to show God's power and defeat Baal worshippers. Jezebel got mad and wanted to kill every prophet, so Elijah requested that God let him die, and he ran away and hid in a cave. He was alone and lonely. God went after him and asked Elijah why he was hiding in the cave. Elijah replied that he was the only prophet left. God told him there were 7,000 left. Even so, it is easy to understand how there are times when the enemy can make you feel worthless and left hung out to dry. This is especially true after the loss of a loved one if you're living in a home all by yourself. Days feel longer and the nights feel like they will never end. Loneliness even occurs when you pastor a church and you feel everyone is against you, that you are standing all alone with no help, no support, no encouragement, no money …

like you're just existing. Loneliness also rears its ugly head when your so-called friends walk away.

When you experience loneliness, remember that Jesus also felt lonely, forsaken, and abandoned. God wants to fellowship with us and wants us to reach out to Him. With God always there waiting for your invitation to spend time, how could you ever be lonely again?

Prayer for Loneliness

Heavenly Father,

There are so many lonely people in this world; they are weary and afflicted. Be gracious to every lonely soul. I pray those who are hurting will find their comfort in You. Set us free today as we stand on your promises that even though mother and father forsake us, and all our friends and loved ones, You promise to never leave us nor forsake us.

I pray that You will deliver me from loneliness as I draw nigh to You. Lift the burden and fill the empty places in my heart with Your great love. Help me to rest in You and be content. Fill me afresh with Your Holy Spirit. Now, I ask that You meet me at the point of my needs.

In Jesus name, Amen.

I will not leave you comfortless: I will come to you.

John 14:18

Let your conversation be without covetousness;
and be content with such things as ye have:
for he hath said, I will never leave thee, nor forsake thee.
So that we may boldly say, The Lord is my helper,
and I will not fear what man shall do unto me.

Hebrews 13:5-6

…and, lo, I am with you always, even
unto the end of the world. Amen.

Matthew 28:20

CHAPTER 3

SCARS OF LOSING A LOVED ONE

And the Lord God said,
It is not good that the man should be alone;
I will make him an help meet for him.

Genesis 2:18

One of the most devastating causes of loss is the death of a loved one. I lost my daughter Crystal at birth many years ago, and recently lost my son. It took years to come to grips with losing Crystal and now the grief of Ronnie, Jr.'s loss is new and raw, and my heart grieves with pangs of sorrow that sometimes take my breath away because he is not beside me. I was used to seeing him and talking with him and enjoying the fellowship and camaraderie of a father and his son, as well as being brothers in the Lord. Now that space he filled is empty and with it comes a sense of loss (or feeling lost) that is hard to describe. Some say losing a child is harder than losing a husband or wife because you bring children into the world, and mold their characters and bring them up in the nurture and admonition of the Lord, protect them, care for their needs, and love them unconditionally from birth. The heartache of losing my children was and is overwhelming and hard to talk about. Merriam-Webster has several definitions for *scar* and two of them are appropriate for these losses: *a lasting moral or emotional injury* and *a mark left on a stem or branch where a leaf or fruit has separated.* These children were my fruit, and they have been separated from me and my wife. There are no words to express the depths of sorrow we feel in relation to them. Because we are mortal and it is appointed unto man once to die, we have no choice but to bear the scars of our loss.

But God reminds us to choose life over grief in our desert of loss. Grief may make those around us uncomfortable, but it does not make God uncomfortable. Despair does not come from God. When Jesus left the earth, He sent another to be the Comforter.

And I will pray the Father, and he shall give you another Comforter, that he may abide with you for ever;

John 14:16

Losing a parent is devastating and can take years to get used to, but losing a husband or wife is another life-altering scar that can lead to acute and chronic depression. When your spouse is no longer there, whether you have been married a year or seventy years, a sadness permeates your existence, takes up residence, and is hard to evict. I heard one woman describe her feelings as living someone else's life, waiting to breathe again, wondering if anything would ever be okay again, and looking forward to heaven because her husband was there. She was not suicidal, and she realized that it was not healthy to want to die prematurely so that she could be with him sooner. She knew that the right reason to want to be in heaven was to be with the Lord forevermore. However, the grief caused her to think unscriptural thoughts and lose her focus for a while. Be careful of the thoughts you let enter your mind – don't make room for the devil and his spirits. Satan is always looking for an opening. He goes to and fro upon the earth seeking whom he may devour. Don't let your loss make you a target; manage your thought life and think godly thoughts.

Finally, brethren, whatsoever things are true, whatsoever things are honest, whatsoever things are just, whatsoever things are pure, whatsoever things are lovely, whatsoever things are of good report; if there be any virtue, and if there be any praise, think on these things.

Philippians 4:8

Loss occurs in many arenas besides death, but sometimes you think the circumstances feel worse than death, especially when a relationship or marriage breaks up. Whereas death is final and there is no other choice, a broken relationship carries with it some special kinds of loss and stress. It often leaves you in limbo and wondering if you will get back together, if the breach can be repaired, if you should go back or move on, and many other considerations that keep your emotions sore and throbbing. Your self-esteem suffers, your concentration is gone, and your ability to function in daily life is often damaged. You sometimes wonder if you are "good enough" for anyone else after this person left you. You wonder why anyone else would want you if you were not good enough to keep. Take those cares to God in prayer and let Him minister to your broken spirit.

He healeth the broken in heart,
and bindeth up their wounds.

Psalm 147:3

Those wounds will eventually become scars. There is a saying that time heals all wounds, but that is not accurate. Time can dull the pain of old wounds, but only Jesus Christ can heal all wounds. He is the Great Physician – the Great Healer – and the grief process is for our healing. We must go through it to get to the other side. In Robert Lowry's song, *Nothing But the Blood of Jesus* (1876), the lyrics ask and answer:

What can make me whole again?
Nothing but the blood of Jesus.

People seek relief from the pain of loss in lots of unhealthy ways: unhealthy for their bodies, unhealthy for their finances, or unhealthy for their spiritual growth. Some try to ignore their loss and jump into new relationships before the scars have healed. Others try to run away from the pain with drugs, alcohol, and other addictions. Still others turn to illicit sexual encounters and risky behaviors to take their minds away from their grief. And there are some who try to replace their loss with "things" and spend money they don't have and accumulate debt trying to appease their sense of loss by going on a buying spree, and some become hoarders. Acquiring things will not assuage your loss. Running away will not work for long, and new relationships before you heal from the old ones will result in repeating the mistakes of the past. So, what should you do? Allow yourself time to mourn, to grieve your loss, and to get alone with God and pour your heart out to Him and let Him speak healing into your spirit.

Blessed are they that mourn: for they shall be comforted.
Matthew 5:4

You may have wondered how to grieve. There is no right way to grieve and throughout history, people have grieved in different ways. The Bible tells of many ways people grieved loss. Some shaved their heads. Job grieved with sackcloth (rough scratchy cloth made of camel or goat hair) and ashes. His friends wept loudly and tore their clothes and put dust on their heads. In the Book of Esther, Mordecai did all three when he heard of the plan to annihilate the Jews. When the Jews found out, they responded with fasting, mourning, wailing, weeping, and sackcloth and ashes. In each of these examples, people reacted to their grief with humility. All these examples are from the Old Testament, but the New Testament says:

Humble yourselves therefore under the mighty hand of God,
that he may exalt you in due time:
Casting all your care upon him; for he careth for you.
1 Peter 5:6-7

How long it takes to grieve a loss depends on the circumstances. There is no right or wrong amount of time. The Bible lists different amounts of time when people died. For example, when Saul died, mourning lasted only seven days. But when Jacob died, it was seventy days – ten times longer than Saul. When Moses died, it was thirty days, then God told Joshua to move on. He also told Joshua:

Have not I commanded thee?
Be strong and of a good courage;
be not afraid, neither be thou dismayed:
for the Lord thy God is with thee whithersoever thou goest.

Joshua 1:9

The Bible is replete with examples of loss. King David's baby son by Bathsheba became very sick. David sought the Lord and lay prostrate before Him all night and prayed and fasted for seven days. On the seventh day, the baby died. His servants were afraid to tell him, but from their whispering, David guessed it and they confirmed that the child had passed away. The servants feared what David might do and were surprised to see David get up, clean up, change clothes, anoint himself, and then eat. They asked him why. His answer is telling of where David's heart was:

And he said, While the child was yet alive,
I fasted and wept: for I said, Who can tell whether
God will be gracious to me, that the child may live?
But now he is dead, wherefore should I fast?
can I bring him back again? I shall go to him,
but he shall not return to me.

2 Samuel 12:22-23

David lost another son he loved, Absalom, who was killed by Joab. David's grief was obvious:

And the king was much moved, and went up to the
chamber over the gate, and wept: and as he went, thus he
said, O my son Absalom, my son, my son Absalom! would
God I had died for thee, O Absalom, my son, my son!

2 Samuel 18:33

Grieving loss is normal, and it is a process, and there are many ways to grieve. You are not just grieving the loss; you are grieving the past, the present, and the future you shared or would have shared together. That is a lot to process and get through and it doesn't happen overnight. Give it all the time you need, and don't let anyone tell you how long it should take. Only you and God know that answer. It comes in waves and you must deal with it as it comes. Grief will return on holidays, birthdays, anniversaries, and other special days. A friend who recently lost her husband told me that her hardest day would be Veterans Day because both she and her husband were veterans and both were very patriotic all year long, but Veterans Day was their special day to share together and reflect on their military careers and stories.

There is no certain way to deal with grief. God has to help you through it because you cannot get over it alone. You must depend on the Holy Spirit to comfort you and listen for that still small voice to encourage you when it is time to move forward. Without the Holy Spirit, we would not be able to handle the stress of loss. Without the reassurance that we will see our Christian loved ones again in heaven, surviving the loss would be even more painful because there would be no hope of joining them in eternity. Aren't you glad you are a Christian? Aren't you blessed that Jesus saved you by His blood atonement on the Cross? Don't you find peace in knowing that the separation is only temporary?

PRAYER FOR LOSS OF LOVED ONES AND GRIEF

Oh Lord, You are my rock and fortress, You are my Creator, You know me better than anyone. I invite You Holy Spirit to send Your comfort. Help me to grieve in a manner that doesn't consume me or keep me bound. Strengthen me, Lord Jesus, to get through it. Give me peace in the midst of my tears and grief. When I feel overwhelmed with pain remind me that you never sleep. Show me healthy ways to honor the memory of my loved one, and ways that glorifies You.

Help me to know that You are here with me during this time of bereavement. Please provide comfort for me like only you can in this difficult time. In Jesus name, Amen.

CHAPTER 4

SCARS OF HUMILIATION

Wherefore Hanun took David's servants,
and shaved off the one half
of their beards, and cut off their garments in the middle,
even to their buttocks, and sent them away.
When they told it unto David, he sent to meet them,
because the men were greatly ashamed:
and the king said, Tarry at Jericho
until your beards be grown, and then return.

2 Samuel 10:4-5

In this Scripture, the men under King David's command were humiliated by the Ammonite King Hanun, who had allied himself with David's enemies and took pleasure in humiliating David's servants. To cut off or shave their beards was an indignity of the worst kind – similar in severity to flogging. But to only cut off half their beards? Hanun no doubt felt proud of himself that he had dishonored, embarrassed, and disgraced King David. Hanum cut off their garments. Remember that in the desert, men in those days wore long gowns and no underwear. To cut off their clothes and expose their backsides would have been mortifying. The enemy accomplished the degradation he sought, but David was a kind ruler and told his men to lay low at Jericho and wait until their beards grew back so they would not be further embarrassed.

David may have understood back then what we know now – humiliation is a deep scar to bear because it has to do with other people's actions and words. We don't necessarily have to do anything to cause humiliation. Whoever said, "sticks and stones may break my bones, but words will never hurt me" was obviously deaf. Words do hurt and they leave indelible and lasting scars on our hearts and minds, and actions speak louder than words.

Humiliation can become a way of life and often starts in childhood with bullying from family members or from kids at school. As it continues, our self-images change to take on the characteristics and accusations blurted out in harsh taunting. If we are constantly assailed with comments about our looks, weight, personality, intelligence, or desirability, we start to believe them and they change our lives, but not for the better.

As we get older, our spirits can be permanently damaged by others' careless or intentional words and actions meant to get even with us or make us jealous. Some want to teach us a lesson we will never forget and go about doing anything and everything possible to cause us to lose face and feel less than who we are. Many do it in public, which is doubly humiliating. We often blame ourselves for the heartless acts of others and over time come to believe that we deserve the cruelty shown to us and that somehow, we are responsible for it. We become depressed and feel hopeless and helpless, don't stand up for ourselves, and get stuck with our lots in life believing there is nothing we can do about it.

Does the above describe you? Are you being humiliated by someone and making excuses for their behavior toward you? Are you being embarrassed in public or in front of your family and friends? Is someone in your life taking away your dignity or undermining your self-worth? Cheating on you? Shaming you for who you are? Humiliations like these are forms of abuse.

None of us are perfect, but we are all loved by our Creator. We deserve to be cared for and treated with respect. Jesus didn't suffer humiliation and die on that lonely Cross so that we would be mistreated, humiliated, or put down. We are made in God's image. We have the seeds of greatness within us. We are children of the Most High God, heirs of salvation with

Christ, and part of God's family. We were adopted into the God of the Universe's household. We are indwelled by the Holy Spirit and are here on a mission from God. We all have a unique purpose and are fearfully and wonderfully made.

I will praise thee; for I am fearfully and
wonderfully made: marvellous are thy works;
and that my soul knoweth right well.
Psalm 139:14

The humiliation you have experienced is part of your scar story and if you let Him, God can use it for good to help others who are walking the same road you have been down.

And we know that all things work together
for good to them that love God, to them who
are the called according to his purpose.
Romans 8:28

SCAR OF HUMILIATION PRAYER

Dear Lord,

Today I command that every shame, disgrace, and the reproach of my life and my family be terminated by force by fire. Lord, I lay before you the memories that still haunt me. Today, I release it and them to You. I draw nigh to You today, and as promised in Your Word, You will draw nigh to me. I declare this day that You are my Healer, my Deliverer, my Redeemer, and my Comforter. I let go of the past so that I can fully embrace my future. In Jesus' name I pray, Amen.

Fear not; for thou shalt not be ashamed:
neither be thou confounded;
for thou shalt not be put to shame: for thou
shalt forget the shame of thy youth,
and shalt not remember the reproach
of thy widowhood any more.

Isaiah 54:4

CHAPTER 5

SCARS OF SHAME AND GUILT

For mine iniquities are gone over mine head:
as an heavy burden they are too heavy for me.

Psalm 38:4

Shame and guilt are not the same. *Guilt* has to do with what we have done or said that was wrong, or what we should have done or said and didn't. It has to do with our actions. Guilt can hold on for years and keep coming back to remind us of what we have done. *Shame* has to do with our concept of who we are inside and how we measure up to the standards of the world we live in. Society places expectations on us about how we should be, act, think, and behave. When our perceptions of ourselves fall short, don't match the imaginary standards, and we don't measure up, we feel ashamed. Actions we feel guilty about can add to our shame and the two can work together to cause depression, lead to addiction, or create stress that causes us to act out even more. As children of God, we must get a handle on guilt and shame if we are to accomplish what He has set before us as His plan for our lives.

Admit it. You have done and said things that you wish you could take back. Lurking in your distant (or not so distant) past are memories of what you should have done differently. These memories gnaw at you and make you feel guilty. Guilt is internally painful and not easy to share.

Let's be honest about it – sometimes it is difficult to be transparent and hard to be vulnerable. It is hard to tell the truth about our lives and admit we hurt. There are times when we just miss the boat, and the pain we experience is self-inflicted. We caused it. No one forced us to do what we did or made us say what we said or made us go where we went. We did it on our own, made our own mess, and are living with the consequences. Let's make it more personal. What might that look like in your life? You might have been caught in the lie, had your deception discovered, or made a fool out of yourself. Could it be that you caused the divorce? Committed adultery? Stole the money? Didn't follow the doctor's advice and now are sicker? Manipulated or bullied? Operated under the Jezebel spirit of sexual immorality? Whatever the case, you are the reason you are in the condition you are in.

The Bible is full of stories of people who bore the scars of their indiscretions, but one that stands front and center is King David. He was a man after God's heart. He loved God and praised Him, wrote psalms to worship Him, and never took his blessings for granted. But David was flawed. He had a problem with lust. The Bible tells of eight of his wives by name (Micah, Abigail, Bathsheba, Ahinoam, Maacah, Haggith, Abital, and Eglah) but he had others as well. Polygamy was acceptable in those days, and all those wives were fine – except for Bathsheba. You know his story. He ate the forbidden fruit of having sex with another man's wife, got her pregnant, then tried to cover it up. When he couldn't, he arranged to have Uriah killed in battle.

Fast forward through the rest of David's life. The baby died. Later his son Amnon picked up the family trait and became enamored with his stepsister Tamar and raped her, shaming both her and the family. David's other son Absalom, Tamar's brother by the same mother, was enraged and after two years of seething in anger, plotted and had Amnon killed. Absalom ran away and stayed gone for a few years. He came back and eventually got cocky and thought he would make a better ruler, so sweet-talked the people and then declared himself king. This time David ran. The conflict eventually came to a battle between David's army and Absalom's followers. David instructed his men to be kind to Absalom for the king's sake, but they didn't listen, and Absalom was killed. Do you think your family has guilt, shame, secrets, and drama? This was a man after God's heart! He lost a son, had a daughter shamed, lost another son, almost lost his kingdom from within his own family, and lost a third son.

Not all bad choices end in disaster, at least not in the long run. Jonah was a minor prophet whom God sent to Nineveh to warn them of impending destruction. Nineveh was the headquarters of the Assyrian empire. The Assyrians had taken captives of the several of the tribes of northern Israel and sent them into exile. The remaining tribes held their breath waiting for the enemy armies to come for them, too. The Assyrians were brutal, pagan, and feared. When their moral sins reached the level of depravity, God planned to destroy them if they didn't straighten up. But like a merciful God who didn't want any to perish, He sent His prophet Jonah to warn them to get their act together.

Jonah didn't want to save the Assyrians from God's wrath. They were heartless, cruel opponents and Jonah wanted them to be destroyed. Instead of being obedient and going to Nineveh, he boarded a ship to Tarshish and went the other way. He wasn't afraid to go to Nineveh; he just didn't want God to forgive His or Jonah's enemies. After all, they had inflicted great pain on the Israelites. They deserved to be punished, didn't they? They didn't deserve God's mercy and forgiveness, did they? Jonah's rebellion caused problems for the crew of the ship. God sent a great storm and the crew thought they would be killed. They sensed it was not a normal storm, but one sent by God to get their attention. They confronted Jonah who confessed that the storm was caused by his disobedience. By mutual consent, the crew threw Jonah overboard, the storm stopped, the seas calmed, and Jonah was in the water alone. Well, not quite alone. God sent a big fish to swallow up Jonah. Without God's intervention, Jonah would have been fish dung on the bottom of the sea. Instead, Jonah sat in the belly of the big fish for three days, unharmed except for his dignity. It would have been dark, maybe cold, and filled with gastrointestinal juices. Yuck! Finally, he cried out to God that he would go to Nineveh. The big fish vomited him up on the banks of the water, complete with seaweed and slime all over him. How disgusting! Why did he wait three days to repent? He could have been on solid ground a lot sooner if not for his stubborn rebellious nature and actions. We do the same thing. We wallow in the slime of our sins and wait for something major to give us an adjustment and change the trajectory of our lives, all the time knowing we are guilty of doing wrong.

Jonah did go to Nineveh, but only delivered a minimal sermon: five words in Hebrew. The gist was that in forty days, Nineveh would be overturned. Maybe secretly Jonah hoped the Ninevites would ignore him and God would still destroy them. But that didn't happen. The king of Nineveh declared a fast, sat in sackcloth and ashes, and decreed that all men and beasts would be covered with sackcloth. Even the cows had to repent and fast. Don't you know that made Jonah mad? He sulked, pouted, and accused God of being too forgiving. Even through Jonah's stubbornness and rebellion, God saved over 120,000 people (and many cows) alive. He can use us all, even with our less than perfect attitudes and actions – even in our guilt and shame.

There is therefore now no condemnation to
them which are in Christ Jesus, who walk
not after the flesh, but after the Spirit.

Romans 8:1

The good news is that you don't have to remain under the condemnation of guilt or shame. God forgives our past, present, and future. He puts our sins behind His back, throws them as far as the east is from the west, and buries them in the sea.

Behold, for peace I had great bitterness:
but thou hast in love to my soul delivered it
from the pit of corruption: for thou hast
cast all my sins behind thy back.

Isaiah 38:17

If God doesn't remember our sins, who are we to keep picking them up? Who has the right to keep accusing us of past mistakes? Those accusations from ourselves and others are not of God. The devil is the

accuser of the brethren, and he loves to remind us of our past and keep
our guilt and shame churning, so we are useless for the Kingdom. Don't
let that happen!

*As far as the east is from the west,
so far hath he removed our transgressions from us.*

Psalm 103:12

So, you did it. You sinned. You caused your own heartache and
embarrassment. What next? Admit it, face it, make amends if you can,
ask for forgiveness from God, the people you harmed, and yourself. You
will always carry the scars, but they can serve as reminders of God's
mercy and forgiveness. It is okay to show the scars to others. Our scar
stories can help others along the way going through the same thing.
We can have the scar without the guilt of what we did to get the scar.
God forgives the sin. As Joel Osteen says, "Guilt doesn't do anything
productive, it causes you to struggle more … Guilt will keep you from
your destiny."

*If we confess our sins, he is faithful
and just to forgive us our sins,
and to cleanse us from all unrighteousness.*

1 John 1:9

PRAYER TO RELEASE GUILT AND SHAME

Dear Lord,

I open my heart to you completely. You know I feel like I've made many mistakes and I feel very bad about my actions and my mistakes. I need your help in letting go of the shame and guilt instead of beating myself up about them. Deliver me from reminders that still hurt, torment, and control me. My poor choices in the past don't define who I am. So today, I declare healing and wholeness. Now, I pray that your love flows into every cell of my body and to the very depths of my soul to cleanse and restore me to wholeness. I declare, "I am not what I've done," in Jesus name.

For God did not send his son into the world to condemn you,
but that the world through him might be saved.

John 3:17

CHAPTER 6

SCARS OF BETRAYAL

For it was not an enemy that reproached me;
then I could have borne it: neither was it he that
hated me that did magnify himself against me;
then I would have hid myself from him:
But it was thou, a man mine equal, my
guide, and mine acquaintance.
We took sweet counsel together, and walked
unto the house of God in company.

Psalm 55:12-14

O f all the wounds we endure with their resulting scars, betrayal may be the worst. Why? Because an enemy cannot betray us, neither can a stranger. Those we know, trust, and confide in are the culprits who can hurt us the most and worst. The pain can be acute, intense, and last a long time with waves that wash over into all areas of our lives.

Betrayal is hard to shake off and even harder to bounce back from once it occurs. We no longer know who we can trust, so we remain guarded and unwilling to let others into our personal space for fear of similar betrayal. We don't open up to others because we know what can happen because it already has. We experience anger, outrage, grief, and sadness simultaneously. Our souls have holes in them that cannot be mended. We have a deep longing to be healed, but even as our souls groan for transformation, we shut out the world because we don't want to take the chance that we will be betrayed again.

Sound familiar? Betrayal shows up in many ways and from many directions. Here are some examples:

1. Your spouse can cheat on you emotionally and physically, withhold love and acceptance, use your children against you, lie to you, talk about you behind your back, refuse to put effort into your relationship to keep it alive and happy, or withdraw from you in day-to-day life. All of these are forms of betrayal of marriage vows and cause deep pain.

2. Your parent(s) can betray your trust by not taking care of you, showing favoritism, neglecting you, abusing or molesting you, or just not being present in the moment. These betrayals start in childhood, make you feel like damaged goods, and have effects that follow you into adulthood and cause relationship problems unless you come to grips with them.

3. Friends or family can betray your trust by revealing secrets you confided.

4. Your boyfriend, girlfriend, or fiancé can betray you by cheating on you, putting his or her friends above you in importance, or intentionally neglecting you.

5. Your loved ones and friends can betray you by stealing from you, plotting against you, talking about you behind your back, telling lies about you, turning their backs on you when you need them desperately, or failing to be supportive influences in your life.

6. Your boss or coworkers can betray you by blaming you for things you didn't do, stealing a promotion or giving a promotion to someone else when you deserve it, being abusive to you in terms of dumping their work on you and treating you without respect, punishing you for speaking your mind when something is wrong, sexually or verbally harassing you, or taking credit for your ideas and efforts.

7. Your mentor that you have looked up to for a long time betrays you by behaving in a manner that completely contradicts everything they stand for and value in life.

The list could go on and on. No one is immune from betrayal and when it occurs, it is shocking and hard to accept when the other face of the two-faced person comes to light. The wounds and scars can last a lifetime.

Betrayal has widespread effects, and the process of healing is similar to the process of healing from grief and loss. There are five well-known stages of grief developed by Elizabeth Kubler-Ross (1973):

1. Denial
2. Anger
3. Bargaining
4. Depression
5. And finally, Acceptance.

Betrayal is a form of loss and it causes grief. We don't always go through the stages in order, and we tend to cycle through the stages, go back to a stage, then cycle through again. Let's talk about these stages.

When in denial, we can't believe the betrayal happened; we can't believe he or she cheated on us or lied to or about us, left us, or whatever the situation may be. Denial comes from the initial shock and the unwillingness to believe that someone we loved and cared about was capable and willing to hurt us intentionally. We also don't want to believe that we let it happen, that we were naïve enough not to see it coming, that we trusted without question, or that we shared without thought of being humiliated. Denial is about people who betrayed us, but also about us being the recipients of their deliberate betrayal.

When we stop denying the situation, then we get mad. Anger is normal and acceptable and necessary to the healing process. It is okay to get mad! The Bible tells us:

Be ye angry, and sin not:
let not the sun go down upon your wrath:
Neither give place to the devil.

Ephesians 4:26 – 27

In other words, be careful what you do and say when angry, and don't hold onto the anger – let it go. Easier said than done, but with God's help, you can do it. That doesn't mean the anger will not return for another round or two later, but you can win the battle against fury and indignation and overcome the temptation to sin while angry. Jonah had a hard time letting go of his anger and indignation when God spared the Ninevites:

And God said to Jonah, Doest thou
well to be angry for the gourd?
And he said, I do well to be angry, even unto death.

Jonah 4:9

I don't know about you, but I am very glad that God doesn't hold onto anger. He doesn't want us to keep it either; we need to let go of it, even if it means we have to experience the pain that often replaces the emotional space that anger previously filled.

Next comes bargaining. Have you ever begged or tried to negotiate while trying to get a situation corrected? For instance, if a spouse or loved one left you, have you ever begged them for another chance? Told them you would change even if you were not the problem? Begged them to come back? Made deals of "if you do this, then I will do that" or something similar? If so, then you understand the nature of bargaining. It is a last-ditch effort to postpone the inevitable in a bad situation or relationship. In the case of grief and loss, it normally takes the form of trying to bargain with God to postpone or cancel an outcome that is obvious.

Moses tried to bargain with God when he came down from Mount Sinai and found that the Hebrew children and his brother Aaron had made a golden calf and were partying and worshipping the calf. That must have been a huge betrayal of Moses' trust, but he still petitioned God and bargained for God to forgive them:

Yet now, if thou wilt forgive their sin--;
and if not, blot me, I pray thee, out of thy
book which thou hast written.

Exodus 32:32

When bargaining doesn't work, and anger subsides, and denial is history, depression sets in. Unlike normal sadness, which is usually temporary and transient, depression can be chronic or acute, long-lasting, and have physical, emotional, psychological, and mental manifestations. When you are around a depressed person, you know it right away. You notice their countenance is sluggish. They lack energy, have flat affect (don't seem to experience joy or excitement), have a negative outlook on life, can't seem to get in gear and are stuck in limbo, are unconcerned about their appearance or health, lack interest in doing anything or being part of anything (sometimes including family), and can't think about the future or make plans. Depression is not a lost subject in the Bible. Proverbs 12:25 tells us:

Heaviness in the heart of man maketh it
stoop: but a good word maketh it glad.

Many of the psalms address depression, but none so eloquently as when David wrote:

Why art thou cast down, O my soul?
and why art thou disquieted in me?
hope thou in God: for I shall yet praise him
for the help of his countenance.

Psalm 42:5

Patriarchs of the faith were not exempt from depression. You could hear the despair in Jeremiah's voice when he said:

Cursed be the day wherein I was born: let not the
day wherein my mother bare me be blessed.
Jeremiah 20:14

The mighty man of God, Elijah, was not without his moments of depression:

But he himself went a day's journey into the wilderness,
and came and sat down under a juniper tree:
and he requested for himself that he might die;
and said, It is enough; now, O Lord, take away
my life; for I am not better than my fathers.
1 Kings 19:4

If anyone had a right to be depressed, it was Job. We find that he repeatedly addressed his despair, but expressed his suffering and anguish when in Job 10:1, he said:

My soul is weary of my life; I will leave my complaint
upon myself; I will speak in the bitterness of my soul.

There are many other examples of betrayals in the Bible: David, Joshua, Sampson, and Abner, to name a few.

Jesus was familiar with grief and certainly with betrayal. He talked with, traveled with, and lived with His disciples, and yet Judas still sold him out for thirty pieces of silver. In the end, Judas realized what he had done and tried to return the money, knowing he had betrayed innocent blood. The Pharisees would not take the money back, and Judas was so depressed that he took his own life. Jesus was betrayed by Peter who denied Him three times. He knew he had to face the Cross, and He wasn't looking forward to it. He was willing to do it for our salvation, but it caused him to sweat drops of blood.

He is despised and rejected of men; a man of sorrows,
and acquainted with grief: and we hid as it were our faces
from him; he was despised, and we esteemed him not.

Isaiah 53:3

The final stage is acceptance. We have to face and accept the reality of the betrayal and although we may never be alright with it, at least we can acknowledge it, accept it, and try to move on. We may go back and forth several times through the other stages before we land in stage five and stay there. It is an ongoing process. I wish I could tell you that there are shortcuts, but there are no easy fixes and no way to circumvent the process of healing when we have been betrayed and suffer the loss and grief that results. The process can be slow. But there are some steps you can take to start the transformation, lessen the pain, and start the healing process:

1. Begin by acknowledging that it occurred. It is what it is and denying it won't change that.
2. Release the whole situation to God. In the Bible, David frequently took his scars, wounds, complaints, depression, despair, loneliness, and sense of being wronged and gave them to God. He did not complain to others; he went to the source of healing and made his petitions known to God.
3. Know that God will take care of your enemies. You do not need to seek revenge or get even. Romans 12:19 tells us that, "Vengeance is mine; I will repay, saith the Lord." Also remember that when God is fighting your battles for you, He is simultaneously looking out for you and your best interests.

As for me, I will call upon God; and the Lord shall
save me. Evening, and morning, and at noon,
will I pray, and cry aloud: and he shall hear my voice.
He hath delivered my soul in peace from the battle
that was against me: for there were many with me.

Psalm 55:16-18

BETRAYAL: PRAYER FOR BROKEN TRUST

Lord God of Heaven, as I move forward, heal me from a broken heart. Help me to have healthy relationships, and not to punish those who have goodwill towards me by assuming that they will betray me like people in the past have done. Lord, give me grace to forgive so that I will not harbor anger, bitterness, or hatred. Take away any discouragement I feel and replace it with hopeful confidence that I can learn to trust again. Help me to rebuild trust again in relationships of the ones who hurt me if they choose to reconcile again. I choose to forgive, and I open my heart to receive your healing and declare that I will trust again.

I need your grace and ask that You rule in every area of my life. Thank you, Lord.

CHAPTER 7

SCARS OF RAPE AND MOLESTATION

But if a man find a betrothed damsel in the field,
and the man force her, and lie with her: then
the man only that lay with her shall die.

Deuteronomy 22:25

R ape and molestation are crimes – against the law. It has been so
since the early days in the Bible. Prohibitions and punishment
for rape were found in the Torah (also known as the Pentateuch),
the first five books of the Bible, which were delivered as edicts by Moses
to the Hebrews while in the desert. When a woman was raped, the man
was killed. Even though it was not the woman's fault, in that culture,
the woman was shamed and would never marry, have children, or be
in a relationship. She was spoiled goods and was not wanted by a man
afterward. That was Tamar's fate. Even though she was King David's
daughter, came from royalty on her mother's side, and was as beautiful as
her brother Absalom, she was shamed and disgraced by her stepbrother
Amnon who raped her, then refused to look at her, acknowledge her, or
even be in the same room with her. Her life was ruined.

We don't live in those times anymore, and women (and men!) who
have been molested or raped can have relationships, get married, and
have children. Some things have not changed, though. The stigma of

being damaged goods still rests in the hearts of those violated. Society has come a long way in efforts to stop blaming the victim, but the inward scars of being raped or molested linger. Some do not report the assault for fear of retaliation or not being believed or being judged or blamed. The physical trauma is bad enough, but emotional trauma is heaped up to devastating when those who have been raped or molested are met with doubt about their credibility. Many victims blame themselves and think that they should have been able to stop it, or that they somehow deserved it or it would not have happened to them. They feel guilt, shame, or both.

The truth is that rape and molestation are sexual violence and they are not really about sex; they are about control and power. Sex is just the medium to exercise that power. Rape victims feel powerless and dominated, as well as humiliated, debased, and cheapened. Victims may hate their bodies and may take showers and baths constantly to try to wash away the shame because they feel dirty. They may have flashbacks and nightmares, and often don't feel safe. Even though this crime happened *to* them, it was not *about* them. That fact does not make it any easier or less traumatic for victims, whose relationships may suffer after rape or molestation, even if their loved ones provide support and let them know they are still loved.

The Bible addresses sexual assault in a consistent manner throughout. Deuteronomy tells us that the attacker is as guilty as if he had killed someone, but the woman is without guilt or fault:

> *But if a man find a betrothed damsel in the field,*
> *and the man force her, and lie with her: then*
> *the man only that lay with her shall die.*
> *But unto the damsel thou shalt do nothing;*
> *there is in the damsel no sin worthy of death:*
> *for as when a man riseth against his neighbour,*
> *and slayeth him, even so is this matter:*
> Deuteronomy 22:25 - 26

God has always been on the victim's side in cases of sexual violence and has never accused the woman (or man if that is the case) of being promiscuous or bringing on the attack from her (his) conduct. God's law gives women the benefit of the doubt and doesn't accuse them or shame them. If only the courtrooms of the world were as empathetic and sympathetic to the victim…

According to the Center for Disease Control (CDC), one in five women are sexually assaulted at some point in their lives, and often by someone in their families or someone they know. If you have been sexually assaulted, raped, molested, or harassed, you are not alone. Twenty percent of the women you meet carry wounds and scars from similar trauma. Like you, they hide their scars because they feel ashamed and culpable or responsible for the attack. Those who endured ongoing sexual violence may feel they are not worth anything or stuck in their abusive situation and will never be able to escape. If you were to reveal your scars to them so they could see that you survived, thrived, and overcame your assault, you would give courage and encouragement that might allow them to overcome their trauma. And remember: God is your vindicator and He will never stop loving you, caring for you, and giving you a hope and a future.

Sing, O heavens; and be joyful, O earth;
and break forth into singing, O mountains:
for the Lord hath comforted his people,
and will have mercy upon his afflicted.

Isaiah 49:13

Prayer for Rape/Molestation

Father God of Heaven, in the precious name of Jesus, heal me where I've been hurting a long time. Heal every area of my life: mentally, physically, emotionally, and sexually. Take the painful memories away from childhood to adulthood, in Jesus name.

Sustain me by Your grace, comfort me in my suffering, and help me to remember what You say about me and not the trauma of rape and molestation. Now, renew my strength and give me confidence in the power of Jesus Christ to heal, that even when I am afraid, I will put my whole trust in You. I seek refreshing and peace. Heal the hurt left from trauma as I move forward with expectation because I can rest in certainty of Your healing power. Remind me that I am not what happened to me and it was not my fault. Heal my hurting heart and bind all emotional wounds so that I can live the life that You planned for me with purpose and power.

Give justice to the weak and the orphan.
Maintain the right of the lowly and destitute
Psalm 82:3 (NRSV)

CHAPTER 8

SCARS OF
OFFENSE AND
UNFORGIVENESS

Moreover if thy brother shall trespass against thee,
go and tell him his fault between thee and him alone:
if he shall hear thee, thou hast gained thy brother.

Matthew 18:15

The demon that derails destinies is the spirit of offense. My brothers and sisters, this is a lethal spirit, and it's very dangerous. It will destroy everything that comes in its path like a tornado. The enemy uses this spirit to break up homes, relationships, friendships and even churches. When you investigate the matter, it is always over small things. People get offended over anything today. If you look at them a certain way, if you say something they don't agree with, if you fail to call their name, or if you praise one above another, that is enough to create offense. At other times, you don't have to do anything; they decide they are just going to be offended.

According to Matthew 24, we can see the signs of the last days: wars and rumors of wars, earthquakes in diverse places, and pestilence (such as COVID-19 Coronavirus). In verse 10 it says and many shall be offended and repel, begin to distrust and desert (Him who they ought to trust and obey) and will stumble and fall away and betray one another and pursue one another with hatred. In Luke 17:1-4, Jesus tells us that offenses will come, and we need to forgive quickly. Yes, we will feel offended, but how we deal with it is what matters. When offense shows up, don't act like it's not there. The moment it raises its ugly head, confront it, because this spirit will hinder your walk with God. It will also block the blessings of God. Don't allow the spirit of offense to cut off God's power flowing through you.

Oxford Online Dictionary tells us that the meaning of offense is annoyance or resentment brought about by a perceived insult to or disregard for oneself or one's standards or principles. It can be anger, irritation, wrath, displeasure, disapproval, ill feelings, animosity, opposition and many more. Simply put, means to feel hurt by someone or what they have done or said to you. I know of powerful men and women that missed many opportunities because they allowed a spirit of offense to rule and dictate at crucial points in their lives. I know people who stopped speaking to one another for many years, because of a misunderstanding that could have been settled if they could have put aside the spirit of offense. Instead, they carry the scars of offense.

Please don't take the bait of the enemy when you carry the spirit of offense. The resentment can be triggered by the smallest things. There have been times I preached on a certain subject, and at the end of the service someone would be waiting to talk to me. The first thing out of their mouth was, "I know you were talking about me in that message today." To be honest, I didn't have a clue of what they were referring to or talking about. Listen my friend, you will always have something to be offended about, if you allow yourself to be. Don't allow it! Make up your mind to forgive anyone who causes you to be offended. If you hold on to offense, it will turn into a stronghold, and that's when the devil will eat you for lunch because you just opened the door to uninvited and evil spirits. If you don't repent, it will turn into bitterness and it will destroy you (not the person you have the offense against). Let it go. Don't worry about winning, just settle the score by forgiving, and then you'll be free by the power of God.

There are many examples of the scars of offense in the Bible. We read about King David's son, Absalom, in 2 Samuel, Chapter 13. Absalom was offended and nursed a grievance against Amnon, his half-brother who raped his sister Tamar. Amnon deceived Tamar and took advantage of her. He got her alone, raped her, and then threw her out like garbage. When Absalom learned what happened, he was angry and wanted revenge. His sister was forever tainted, became unfit for marriage in those days, and suffered the humiliation of being used sexually. King David did nothing about it, so Absalom bided his time, and after two years of holding the offense in his heart, he took matters into his own hands. Absalom got Amnon drunk and killed him. Later, Absalom betrayed his father, and was later killed by King David's men. Anywhere there's offense, it leads to betrayal. There are many people who point their offense toward God because they blame Him for:

- Unfulfilled expectations
- Taking away their hope of something
- Loss of a loved one, spouse, child sickness or disease, divorce, or debt
- Their abuse as a child, or
- Any number of other perceived offenses.

In the book of Psalms, David's expressed his feelings of perceived abandonment by God. He felt lonely and helpless at times, even haunted by his enemies.

My God, my God, why hast thou forsaken me?
why art thou so far from helping me,
and from the words of my roaring?
O my God, I cry in the day time, but thou hearest
not; and in the night season, and am not silent.

Psalm 22:1-2

Let's take a look at Job. He lost health, wealth, and family, plus he was tormented by the devil. His body broke out with boils, his friends thought he had secret sin, and his wife told him to curse God and die. But Job didn't get offended with God, or curse God. Instead, he refused to be angry with God:

And said, Naked came I out of my mother's
womb, and naked shall I return thither:
the Lord gave, and the Lord hath taken away;
blessed be the name of the Lord.

Job 1:21

Job's wife might have judged God or carried a spirit of offense against God, but Job knew better and so do we. God is the only one who can forgive us, heal us from a spirit of offense, and use our scars of offense for the Kingdom. The Bible tells us to overlook offenses, and not to allow ourselves to be easily angered. We are instructed operate in self-control and let all the Fruit of the Spirit (love, joy, peace, patience, kindness, goodness, faithfulness, gentleness, and self-control) operate in our lives and not to keep records of wrongs. God will be our judge.

Dearly beloved, avenge not yourselves,
but rather give place unto wrath: for it is written,
Vengeance is mine; I will repay, saith the Lord.

Romans 12:19

We expect people who are different from each other to be offended sometimes, but in this respect, many Christians don't look much different from unbelievers. It is easy to get offended, and easier still to harbor unforgiveness. However, it is not scriptural.

Satan is the father of lies. He comes to steal, kill, and destroy and likes nothing better than to put brothers against brothers, children against parents, husbands against wives, or church members against each other. The spirit of offense seeks to divide God's people and break up the church one incident at a time, one marriage at a time, one relationship at a time. This is not God's will.

He who covers a transgression seeks love,
but he who repeats a matter separates friends.

Proverbs 17:9 (NKJV)

Offense takes away our peace and causes us to divert our attention from the things of God. Instead of thinking on what is lovely, pure, right, and true, offense causes us to dwell on the offense, looks for evidence and proof of continued offense, and increases our fuming and feuding so that it is difficult to see Jesus when someone looks at us. If we let the spirit of offense inhabit our hearts, we cannot forgive. If we choose not to forgive, it is iniquity and therefore sin. Allowing offense to abide in us leads to other sins involving revenge, gossip, rumors, even slander. In addition, unforgiveness can lead to bitterness that poisons our relationships with others and with God. Many churches have divided over rumors, gossip, and choosing sides in arguments that should not have been, because the spirit of offense and unforgiveness was stronger in the body of Christ than the spirit of unity and forgiveness. This is not what God wants from us – He hates it when His children act that way.

These six things doth the Lord hate: yea,
seven are an abomination unto him:
A proud look, a lying tongue, and hands
that shed innocent blood,
An heart that deviseth wicked imaginations,
feet that be swift in running to mischief,
A false witness that speaketh lies, and he
that soweth discord among brethren.

The Bible has much to say about unforgiveness and offense. God does not want us to walk around with a chip on our shoulders, carry anger or malice in our hearts, or waste time being antagonized by people we perceive to have slighted, disrespected, used, cheated, or treated us unfairly. John 17:21 tells us how God wants us to act toward each other:

That they all may be one; as thou,
Father, art in me, and I in thee,
that they also may be one in us: that the world
may believe that thou hast sent me.

How does that apply to us? Don't be so easily offended. We have power in agreement, but there is no power in divisiveness. Besides that, when we are not in agreement, we have broken fellowship with our brother in Christ, but also broken fellowship with God. Refusing to forgive hinders our prayers because God doesn't hear us.

And when ye stand praying, forgive,
if ye have ought against any: that your Father also
which is in heaven may forgive you your trespasses.
Mark 11:25

Consider what eternity would look like if God had remained offended by our sins and refused to forgive us our trespasses. We would die in our sins and spend eternity in hell separated from the Father. But God didn't do that. Instead He sent His only son Jesus to die on a lonely Cross. We continue to sin against God, and He continues to willingly forgive us. We are made in His image and He expects us to also forgive.

Then came Peter to him, and said, Lord, how oft shall
my brother sin against me, and I forgive him?
till seven times? Jesus saith unto him, I say not unto thee,
Until seven times: but, Until seventy times seven.
Matthew 18:21-22

Forgiveness is the basis of Christian faith. We can come boldly to the Throne of Grace and enjoy fellowship. Without the shed blood of Jesus Christ, we would have no fellowship with the Father. We are forgiven of so much and enjoy so great a salvation that God expects us to forgive others their offenses toward us. Matthew 5:25 counsels us to agree with our adversaries quickly.

Is it hard to forgive? Yes. But if we do not forgive, we hurt ourselves more than the person who has offended us. Unforgiveness eats us alive on the inside. The Bible tells us to be angry and sin not, and not to let the sun go down on our anger. There is a good reason for that: It takes a lot of negative emotion to hang onto hurt. The longer we are angry, the more emotion we have invested in the situation and the harder it is to forgive. It becomes a matter of pride to hold onto the offense. Let go of it and ask God to heal you of the hurt, so that your inner peace returns, and fellowship is restored.

Then said Jesus, Father, forgive them;
for they know not what they do.

Luke 23:34

PRAYER FOR OFFENSE

Father, thank you for showing me myself. I acknowledge this area in my life needs to be addressed. Forgive me for carrying the spirit of offense and allowing bitterness to consume me. Expose any hidden unforgiveness or secret offenses. Today, I release it to You, Lord. I thank You for setting me free! Help me to turn my heart toward You – no matter what I have suffered, how long I've suffered, or whose fault it may have been. Give me grace to forgive so I will not harbor anger or pain, seek revenge, or insist on finding justice for my hurt. Lord, my Rock and Redeemer, I confess that I need You. Today, I acknowledge it, and I give it to You.

Be ye angry, and sin not: let not the sun
go down upon your wrath:
Ephesians 4:26

For if ye forgive men their trespasses, your
heavenly Father will also forgive you:
Matthew 6:14

CHAPTER 9

SCARS OF REGRET

*So the LORD said, "I will wipe from the face of the
earth the human race I have created--and with them
the animals, the birds and the creatures that move along
the ground--for I regret that I have made them."*

Genesis 6:7 (NIV)

How many of us wish we could press the rewind button and relive our lives over again? Or perhaps turn back the hands of time? There are many people in this world who live lives of regret. Regret is one of the most frequently experienced emotions and it stems from decisions we make or don't make. It could be a decision about a college, career, or a job opportunity, a marriage partner, expensive purchase, choice of a home, or how many children to have (or not have).

Sometimes we move too quickly without praying about a matter or seeking wisdom. Proverbs 11:14 tells us that there is safety in a multitude of counsel. I remember planting a garden too early without watching the forecast. I planted as soon as the temperature reached 80-degree days. I started planting seed, not knowing there were cold days ahead. As a result, the frost came, and the plants died. I regret starting too soon. My intentions were good, but the regret was still there. It cost me time and money, but I learned from that mistake and didn't repeat it. We all make mistakes (small or large), and if we keep living, we will keep making mistakes. We are human and fallible.

No one is perfect, and it is normal to have regrets – we are all human and have done or failed to do things that in retrospect were not the best choices. Even God had regrets. He regretted having made man when He saw that wickedness prevailed constantly – not because He made a mistake, but because the sin He witnessed caused Him sorrow. God's regret in Hebrew was *ni'ham'ti,* which meant God experienced unhappy emotions. To correct the situation, God sent the Flood.

Later, God gave the Israelites the king they asked for. But Saul turned away from God's ways and failed to follow God's commandments. That disobedience caused God to be grieved and for Him to regret making Saul the king.

> *Then came the word of the Lord unto Samuel, saying,*
> *It repenteth me that I have set up Saul to be king:*
> *for he is turned back from following me,*
> *and hath not performed my commandments.*
> *And it grieved Samuel; and he cried unto the Lord all night.*
>
> 1 Samuel 15:10-11

An Australian nurse, Bronnie Ware, worked with terminally ill people and took note of their wishes right before dying. In her book, *The Top Five Regrets of the Dying – A Life Transformed by the Dearly Dying* (2019), she compiled a list of the top regrets she heard often. They were:

1. **I wish I'd had the courage to live a life true to myself, not the life others expected of me.** She noted that doing at least some of the things you always wanted to do was important, because once your health is gone, it is too late, and regret follows.
2. **I wish I hadn't worked so hard.** Every man she nursed had this regret. She reminds us that money is not as important as the people we love.
3. **I wish I'd had the courage to express my feelings.** Maggie Kuhn's famous quote, "Speak your truth, even if your voice shakes," is true and if you choose your words so as not to inflict unneeded hurt, you can avoid pent up emotions that lead to poor choices and poorer outcomes.

4. **I wish I had stayed in touch with my friends.** Friends taken for granted may not be there when you get around to them.
5. **I wish that I had let myself be happier.** We spend much time doing for others and often forget or don't get around to doing what makes us happy.

I have heard story after story of regrets:

- I wish we had children, or I wish we had more than one child, or wish we would have adopted
- I should have dated this girl or that girl, or this guy or that guy
- Regrets of marrying the wrong person
- Regrets of divorcing more than once.

What do you regret? Sins in your past? Decisions you made? Paths you followed that didn't turn out well? People you hurt? Not spending enough time with your children? Words you said to someone that you wish you could take back? Dropping out of college? Getting divorced? Having an abortion? Taking drugs? Things you didn't do when you still had time to do them? Any or all of these are typical regrets. We all have things that we regret, and given the chance, we would change them for a different outcome. But don't dwell on the regrets. My friend, there will always be room for improvement, and we might always wonder about how our lives would be different if we had taken a different road or made a different choice.

Then there's some people who can't stop hurting over the physical, emotional, spiritual, and mental pain they have caused others. If you are one of those people, you can relive it every day, but you can't undo what's been done. These might include the *should haves*: I should have been a better worker, a better wife, a better husband, a better father or a better friend. A man I know can't enjoy his success because he neglected his family. So now he feels guilty and deals with panic attacks every day. He often wonders why he didn't realize what was happening before this late in life.

Harry Chapin wrote a song called "Cat's In the Cradle" containing a powerful message that relationships are built in small moments over a lifetime, and that you get out of it what you put into it. In the song, the father never had time for his son when the little boy was growing up. The boy would ask, "When you coming home, Dad?" and Dad would answer, "I don't know when, but we'll get together then." However, *then* never came and the boy grew wanting to be just like his father. When Dad finally got time to be with his son, the young man had a family of his own and was too busy for his father. The son always said he wanted to grow up to be just like his dad, and that is exactly what occurred. The father made a series of continual mistakes and no doubt felt guilt from it, and similar situations still happen today.

You can't allow guilt to consume you. You will never have peace as long as you're reminding yourself of your past mistakes, faults, and failures. Don't try to deny them, just confront them and deal with the issues. Confess them and move forward. Use them as stepping stones – not stumbling blocks. You need to decree and declare that "I will not let regret rule over me and suck the joy out of my life. My days of regret are over and done! I acknowledge I missed my moment and I missed a season of my life. I made some bad decisions, but I learned from them."

We cannot change the past, but we can change the future. The Bible tells us:

And we know that all things work together
for good to them that love God,
to them who are the called according to his purpose.

Romans 8:28

Even when we fail and regret the consequences of our actions, God uses those failures for good and makes them part of our testimonies to be witnesses to others. No matter what we have done in the past, God is not through with us. Our actions that cause regret to us are no surprise to God. He didn't get up this morning and say, "Oh no! Look what my child has done." He knew what you would do, He had a plan to turn it to good, and He continues to love you no matter what you did.

The scars of regret will torment you if you let them. But God is not a God of torment, He is a God of peace. You can reconcile your regret in prayer and God will use your circumstances to help others. God has used those recovering from alcohol and drug addiction to help others just starting that journey; those with prison records to start prison ministries; and those who have suffered great loss from their actions to counsel those who have new losses. God still has a plan for your life.

For I know the plans I have for you," declares the LORD,
"plans to prosper you and not to harm you,
plans to give you hope and a future.
Jeremiah 29:11

Prayer for Regret

Dearest Heavenly Father,

I come before You today with sorrow for my actions, and regret in my heart for the poor choices I have made. I also come with a contrite spirit as I realize how my choices have hurt other people – especially those who have loved me no matter what.

Lord, unlike You, I am human and fallable. I have sinned and I am sorry. Please forgive my mistakes and fill me with your righteousness so that when others look at me, they see You instead of my bad choices, poor decisions, and numerous mistakes. Give me peace and rest and release me from the torment of regret that vexes my soul. Restore unto me the joy of thy salvation and be a light to my path so that I have no room for regret in the future. In Jesus' name, Amen.

CHAPTER 10

SCARS OF ADDICTION

There hath no temptation taken you
but such as is common to man: but God is faithful,
who will not suffer you to be tempted above that ye
are able; but will with the temptation also make a
way to escape, that ye may be able to bear it.

1 Corinthians 10:13

I have had many people reach out to me (parents, spouses, family, and friends) who were totally exhausted and at the end of their road, and for some, on the verge of a nervous breakdown. Well my friend, you need to know that you're certainly not the only one who struggles to absorb the hurt and confusion often felt when dealing with their addicted loved ones. At first, family members want to jump in and rescue the person, save him, or fix her, but eventually they realize they can't. Once that sinks in, it feels like hell. Most users know they are not just hurting themselves – they are also hurting everyone connected to them and all who love them.

Addiction is a demanding, seductive, secretive, and cunning behavior. The pain is fueled by crisis after crisis, it's a journey of pain and deception. Most family members and close friends sacrifice their own wellness for the addicted person, and they only end up furthering the addicted person's habit by enabling. Eventually, the enablers become collateral damage, break, and by then, they are depleted of money, strength, patience, and motivation, and they stop enabling the addict. The scars of addiction they carry are not from indulging in drugs or alcohol, but they are no less scarred from being used up.

Once enabling stops, addicts come to themselves and their eyes are opened. One of the first things they realize is all the hurt they have caused family, friends, and loved ones. There are scars of addiction left on recovering addicts. These scars are the physical consequences of the addiction, damage to reputation and health, and realization that they have damaged their own lives through the addictive behaviors. Recovering addicts are scarred psychologically and emotionally; and although they have kicked the habit, they still must deal with the aftereffects.

In the United States, we tend to label chemical abuse and addiction as *disease*. By giving it a medical label, we somewhat release the addict from responsibility because disease is beyond the person's control. Even though they ingested drugs or alcohol to create the chemical-dependent condition, once addicted, society often gives them a pass on accountability.

The Bible has much to say about self-control and accountability. The first Commandment given to Moses was to "have no other gods before me." By putting addiction front and center, and God in the back seat, addicts violate the most basic of Christian doctrines. According to Shaw (2008), addiction in any form (food, sex, pornography, alcohol, drugs, risk-taking behaviors of adrenaline junkies, money, work, sports) is idolatry. You could even classify overuse of social media such as Facebook, Twitter, and Instagram as addictions, and don't forget video games for kids and adults, and compulsive gambling. Except for illicit drugs, none of the addictions are illegal or bad in themselves. It is only when they become obsessive and experiences as a pathological drive to fill our inner void (the void that only God can fill), that they become harmful. We start to desire more intense and acute experiences and after a while, a few drinks or joints are not enough. We need more, then more, then still more to get the same high that a little used to provide. We get tangled up with the world to have peak experiences.

Ye ask, and receive not, because ye ask amiss, that ye
may consume it upon your lusts. Ye adulterers and
adulteresses, know ye not that the friendship of the
world is enmity with God? whosoever therefore will
be a friend of the world is the enemy of God.

James 4:3-4

Idolatry is not a new phenomenon, and there are many biblical accounts of idolatry. One of the most pronounced was while Moses was on Mount Sinai getting The Ten Commandments. The Israelites below, under Aaron's supervision, melted down precious metals and made a golden calf like one in Egypt, and were worshiping it when Moses came back to the camp. Moses destroyed the calf, beat it into powder, mixed it with water, and made the Hebrews drink it. Three thousand people died. Moses destroyed sin from the camp and didn't take any prisoners in his efforts. He dealt with it swiftly and powerfully and let the people know that there was no room for sin among them. This biblical account always amazes me because these people had seen the miraculous hand of God free them, save them, sustain them, and protect them. Yet they still fell into idolatry when they became confused about whether Moses was still alive and coming back.

Lusts of the flesh in the form of addictions go against Scriptures and unchecked, lead to death, which can be in the physical sense, but is, for certain, death in the spiritual sense.

Then when lust hath conceived, it bringeth forth sin:
and sin, when it is finished, bringeth forth death.

James 1:15

Proverbs 23 describes the cycle of repetition in addiction that explains how it works to keep you under its influence:

Who hath woe? who hath sorrow?
Who hath contentions? who hath babbling?
Who hath wounds without cause?

Who hath redness of eyes?
They that tarry long at the wine;
They that go to seek mixed wine.
Look not thou upon the wine when it is red,
When it giveth his colour in the cup,
When it moveth itself aright.
At the last it biteth like a serpent,
And stingeth like an adder.
Thine eyes shall behold strange women,
And thine heart shall utter perverse things.
Yea, thou shalt be as he that lieth
down in the midst of the sea,
Or as he that lieth upon the top of a mast.
They have stricken me, shalt thou say, and I was not sick;
They have beaten me, and I felt it not:
When shall I awake?
I will seek it yet again.

Proverbs 23:29-35

God has the Naloxone for your painkillers of choice, no matter what the source of your pain. When you stop running from God and turn to Him, you will find Him. God didn't move, He is still in the same place, and He will meet you there. By coming back to God, you find a turning point that changes the trajectory of your life and puts you back on solid ground.

O Lord my God, I cried unto thee, and thou hast healed me.
O Lord, thou hast brought up my soul from the grave:
thou hast kept me alive, that I should not go down to the pit.

Psalm 30:2-3

There are many Scriptures that spell out God's power to heal you and help you. Among them are:

Heal me, O Lord, and I shall be healed; save me,
and I shall be saved: for thou art my praise.
Jeremiah 17:14

Then they cry unto the Lord in their trouble,
and he saveth them out of their distresses.
He sent his word, and healed them,
and delivered them from their destructions.
Psalm 107:19-20

And one that gives great hope of relief from the bondage weighing you down in addiction:

Come unto me, all ye that labour and are heavy laden,
and I will give you rest. Take my yoke upon you, and learn of
me; for I am meek and lowly in heart: and ye shall find rest
unto your souls. For my yoke is easy, and my burden is light.
Matthew 11:28-30

Recovering from addiction is a struggle because it has both spiritual and physical components, and both must be treated. The battle is real, and the temptation to relapse is high because your body craves the altered state, and the spirit of addiction wants you back and tries to tempt you. But God does not want you in bondage. He sent His son, Jesus Christ to save you from your sin. Jesus was scourged and His body was beaten for your healing. If only you would have been healed and saved and no one else, Jesus would still have died for your sins. He loves you and He wants you to be whole and well in every way.

Surely he hath borne our griefs, and carried our sorrows:
yet we did esteem him stricken, smitten of God, and afflicted.
But he was wounded for our transgressions,
he was bruised for our iniquities: the chastisement of our
peace was upon him; and with his stripes we are healed.
Isaiah 53:4-5

PRAYER FOR ADDICTION

Lord, thank You for breaking the bondage of addiction off my life. Heal my body, mind, and spirit. Today, I decree that addiction(s) (drugs, alcohol, pornography, food, prescription medication) are a thing of my past and not a part of my future anymore.

Thank you, Lord, that You are my strength and protector, and more powerful than any addiction. Strengthen me in work of recovery and restore any part of my health and heart that have been lost to addiction. When I am weak, please remind me that You are my Rock and Strength. I pray now that the shackles of bondage that have ensnared me be broken off of my life. Through faith, in prayer, I claim freedom from addiction.

I am clean and I am free in Jesus name, Amen.

CHAPTER 11

SCARS OF SUICIDE

The Lord is nigh unto them that are of a broken
heart; and saveth such as be of a contrite spirit.
Many are the afflictions of the righteous: but
the Lord delivereth him out of them all.

Psalm 34:18-19

Suicide is not new. There are seven counts of suicide in the Bible: Abimelech, Sampson, Saul, Saul's armor-bearer, Ahithophel, Zimri, and Judas all took their own lives. Some of them were mighty men of God, some rulers, some men of great renown in their time, and some commoners. Six were in the Old Testament and one in the New Testament. One even walked with Jesus on earth, but still killed himself.

Suicide does not discriminate – it touches people from both sexes, and all walks of life, socioeconomic groups, ages, and physical and mental conditions. There are no "typical" suicides, and sometimes there are no warning signs.

We don't know everything about suicide, but we do know there are some precursors or risk factors that point to the potential for suicide. One of those is suicidal ideation or thinking about killing yourself. Often said in jest (on the surface at least), it is a heads-up to friends and family that something is wrong. Other risk factors are prior suicide attempts; self-inflicted harm and injuries; severe depression; recent loss of a significant person such as parent, child, or spouse; serious injury, illness, or physical pain; alcohol or drug abuse; post-traumatic stress disorder (PTSD) from life trauma or military combat; mental illness;

loss of employment; abuse or neglect; and history of family suicide or the recent suicide of a friend.

It is easy to miss the warning signs of possible suicide, but there are some *tells* that, if present, should cause friends and family concern because the risk is real. These are some of the frequently recognized warning signs from American Foundation of Suicide Prevention (Risk Factors and Warning Signs, 2020):

If a person talks about:

- Killing themselves
- Feeling hopeless
- Having no reason to live
- Being a burden to others
- Feeling trapped
- Unbearable pain

Behaviors that may signal risk, especially if related to a painful event, loss, or change:

- Increased use of alcohol or drugs
- Looking for a way to end their lives, such as searching online for methods
- Withdrawing from activities
- Isolating from family and friends
- Sleeping too much or too little
- Visiting or calling people to say goodbye
- Giving away prized possessions
- Aggression
- Fatigue

People who are considering suicide often display one or more of the following moods:

- Depression
- Anxiety

- Loss of interest
- Irritability
- Humiliation/Shame
- Agitation/Anger
- Relief/Sudden Improvement

Many times, families do not recognize these symptoms until after a person commits suicide, and then the grief is increased because guilt is added. The guilt may be because no one recognized the warning signs, or if the warning signs were known, that no one was able to do anything to stop the suicide before it was too late. It is a terrible, heart-wrenching position for a loved one to be in. For all the recent advances in study of behavior, there is still much the doctors do not understand about the mystery of the phenomenon of people taking their own lives.

Because we are not able to talk to the person who committed suicide, we can only speculate and assume why it happened, and try to put the pieces together. Many professors are trying to chart the process and what they are discovering, especially findings that are on the cutting edge of brain science, may help bring down the toll of suicide in the future. In the meantime, it takes a major toll on families left behind. It leaves many people grieving asking questions that will never be answered, while others blame themselves because they did not know the person was in grief and despair so intense that they were willing to give up their lives to be free of the pain.

When the pain is severe enough, many suicide victims fail to consider the impact their actions will have on those left behind. They just want relief from their pain, and don't realize the amount of pain they will cause others. Suicide leaves a permanent scar that is never erased from the minds of family and friends.

In only one year, I have officiated almost ten suicide funerals. The deceased were young, middle age, and older. There are no words to express how devastated and traumatized the families were in each case. My friend, trying to come up with the right words to comfort family members after a suicide is almost impossible. Families are numb, grief-stricken, and have a thousand unanswered questions. They wonder why the person could not see a way out or find light at the end of the tunnel. They look for warning signs, changes in behavior - anything to try and put the suicide puzzle together.

From 2018 to 2019, I helped with funerals of over 10 people who struggled with the spirit of suicide, and I must tell you it was the most painful experiences I ever had. I spent most of my time counseling and trying to help families make sense of it all. I remember thinking every time that if the person who killed themselves could see what he or she put their families through, they would not have done it. They would not have inflicted such excruciating pain on those who loved them.

I am reminded of a young man who struggled with alcohol abuse. He was in his late twenties, the oldest of six kids from a close-knit loving Christian family. He had four children who adored him. He was divorced but was dating a young woman he hoped to marry. They got in an argument and broke up like many couples do. He was devastated. He started drinking, and then went to the local hardware store, bought a rope, and walked to his father's house. His dad seldom used the garage in wintertime, so the young man slipped in quietly and closed the garage door behind him, barricaded himself in the garage, hung himself from the rafters, and didn't leave a note. No one heard from him for two days, and his family got worried and looked all over town for him. They filed a missing person's report. His car was abandoned. No one had seen him. The family became frantic to find him. They called hospitals and police stations for a hundred miles around. Then his mother noticed that the garage door wasn't closed tightly, and she went in. She found him and had to cut down her own son. Her grief was unbearable and surreal. That was three years ago, and that family has not had a day since that they don't mourn the loss of their son, brother, or father. Their pain is still unreal. The girlfriend was shattered and still cannot date anyone else. His children have nightmares and are not doing well academically or socially in school. A huge hole in the heart of every family member is obvious to any onlooker as they continue to mourn and wonder why.

That was one of many stories of suicide, but even one is too many. One of the questions that families frequently ask is whether suicide sends their lost loved one to hell. I want to take some time to address that question because it is important and relevant.

Sometimes we tend to judge in areas where only God should judge. There are some things we will never know, some answers to questions we may not receive, but secret things belong to God.

The secret things belong unto the Lord our God...
Deuteronomy 29:29

Just remember God is the final judge. Maybe you have had thoughts of harming yourself or ending it all. Please reconsider - cry out for help! Or maybe someone you know is experiencing those thoughts. Here are just a few things to consider doing.

1. Remove yourself from danger. Do not drive, do not stand on a balcony, or be around weapons such as guns, knives, or other potentially harmful objects.
2. Reach out, do not be afraid to ask for help. Reach out to people who care about you and have your best interest at heart. They care about your well being and they want to help you. Your safety is your number one priority, CALL 911. And remember: You can cry out to God first, and you can also cry out to people.

PRAYER FOR SUICIDE

Lord God! Please be with me when I struggle with suicidal thoughts and behavior. Also touch those who have lost a loved one to suicide and continue to need support. Be with me, and help them to know that they are not alone, and they are loved, and that they can look to You when they are in need.

I pray for relief from the strain of mental torment, emotional pressure, and strain of this world. I lay claim to a sound mind. Help me to think on things that are true, noble, just, pure, lovely, of good report, virtuous, and praiseworthy. I reject the enemy's attempt to whisper lies that my life is useless, and things are hopeless.

Lord, be the light that guides me during this time when my mind is overwhelmed with sadness and fear. Give my mind rest and calm my racing thoughts. Give me strength to stand strong in Your promises and believe Your Word. Touch me, dear Lord, with your light, love, and hope. I declare today "I shall live and not die" in Jesus' name.

CHAPTER 12

SCARS OF RACISM

Then Peter opened his mouth, and said,
Of a truth I perceive that God is no respecter of persons:

Acts 10:34

The stories of racism stem from slavery that spanned more than a century, and it left scars in the lives of many African Americans. The effects of those wounds have passed from generation to generation. This painful past and painful history of many (that we thought would be a scar by now), is still an open wound freshly bleeding waiting for closure to happen. Just when we think we've come to the end of racism, it starts all over again. Memories of the past resurface: being gunned down in cold blood, being beaten in the streets, being sprayed by fire hoses, or chased and bitten by dogs, lynched in trees, thrown in rivers, hunted and shot like animals. They have left many scars in the lives of African Americans, but many keep on trusting and believing that we shall overcome some day from:

1. Underground Railroads
2. Montgomery Bus Boycott
3. Selma March
4. Civil War
5. Recent killings.

We could add segregation, Jim Crow, poll taxes, the Little Rock Nine, race wars of the nineteenth century, the assassination of Martin

Luther King, Jr., and race riots of the twentieth century. But it didn't end there – it's been a wound that won't heal. Just recently on CBS news, a mother in New York spoke out about the recent death of George Floyd. As a result of his death, it reopened the long-lasting wounds of the death of her son who was shot by four policemen. Her son was unarmed yet shot fourteen times. He had never been in trouble, so she is mourning all over again. Her pain never goes away; she said this scar will never leave her as long as she lives.

The scars of racism are close to my heart, so close in fact that in 2015, I wrote *Destroying the Root of Racism* in which I championed the solution: Violence begets violence, but unity with the brethren will always invite the Holy Spirit in. I urged those hurt by racism not to let the adversity destroy their character, but instead let it define their character. I want to share some passages from that book that are appropriate to our times (Webb, 2015):

>O-O-O-O<

Racism can be a sneaky sin, and it can take many forms. It can be either seen—as in cases where violence and verbal abuse are present; or unseen— where the sin occurs in the heart and mind without any outward sign. As Christians, we must constantly examine ourselves, checking our thoughts and actions against the Word of God so we don't fall prey to this trap. 1 Corinthians 13:5 says it like this:

"Examine and test and evaluate your own selves to see whether you are holding to your faith and showing the proper fruits of it. Test and prove yourselves. Do you not yourselves realize and know thoroughly by an ever-increasing experience that Jesus Christ is in you—unless you are counterfeits disapproved on trial and rejected." (page 45).

>O-O-O-O<

The issues faced as a victim of racism are extraordinarily similar to those Jesus faced in His own life. The Bible says in Hebrews 4:15,

*For we have not a high priest which cannot be
touched with the feeling of our infirmities;
but was in all points tempted like as we are, yet without sin.*

In Jesus' time, the land was occupied by Rome, a nation which considered Jews to be filth, and Romans persecuted them mercilessly. Not only that, but Jesus was also hated by people of His own race. The people He grew up with rejected and mocked Him. Everywhere He went, He was met with hatred, confrontation, and even violence. Yet in all this, He never once reacted with anger; never once did He try to hurt those who had hurt Him; never once did His character falter. Instead, He exuded love and displayed mercy.

How did He accomplish all of that? We see the answer in John 12:49.

*For I have not spoken of myself; but
the Father which sent me,
he gave me a commandment, what I should say,
and what I should speak.*

Jesus only reacted with love, and only spoke what the Father told Him. He let God guide Him by aligning His character with God's character. Imagine what would happen if more of us lived our lives that way. What would happen if we only spoke from the heart of God? Well, the world would be a lot different. Here is an additional excerpt from *Destroying the Root of Racism* (Webb, 2015):

>=o=o=o=o=<

....*racism is not a one-way street. Whether you're white and hate blacks, black and hate whites, Hispanic and hate Arabs, or Indian and hate Asians, the bottom line is that if you have negative feelings toward other people based on their skin color or nationality, then you are engaging in racism.*

I'm simply just telling it how it is. No matter what race you are, racism is a sin. All too often, it's a sin that goes unchallenged. I applaud those individuals who will stand off in the face of adversity and speak against this immoral behavior. It takes great courage to stand up for what is right (page 14).

>=o=o=o=o=<

He that saith he is in the light, and hateth his brother, is in darkness even until now.
1 John 2:9

Judge not according to the appearance, but judge righteous judgment.
John 7:24

Prayer for Racism

Father God, we come boldly to the Throne of Grace and make our petitions known to You, the Almighty. Although you are no respecter of persons, we live in a world that demonstrates prejudice and racism individually and institutionally. We ask you Father to cleanse our hearts, remove our pain, heal our wounds, and restore our joy. Empower us to be angry and sin not.

The thief comes to steal, kill, and destroy, but Jesus came to give life more abundantly. We praise you and thank you for that abundant life, and for you making our paths straight and not letting any weapon formed against us (including racism) prosper. In Jesus' mighty name, Amen.

CHAPTER 13

SCARS OF ABORTION

There is therefore now no condemnation to
them which are in Christ Jesus, who walk
not after the flesh, but after the Spirit.
For the law of the Spirit of life in Christ Jesus hath
made me free from the law of sin and death.

Romans 8:1-2

O f all the days in a year, Mother's Day is a sad, even scary time, for women who have had abortions. They carry guilt for what they did, shame that they made that choice, and fear that God cannot forgive them for such a grievous sin. They cannot forgive themselves, and that perpetuates the guilt, shame, and fear that can last for decades.

We as a church don't make it any easier. Preachers preach on abortion and call it murder. We all know The Ten Commandments include, "Thou shalt not kill." Women who have had abortions have a hard time accepting God's love and forgiveness when the humans that make up their church family condemn abortion so loudly. These women keep their abortions secret so that they are not humiliated, judged, or looked down on by their sisters and brothers in Christ. But inside, it eats them alive. They fear that their actions will result in them going to hell, or that God will punish them for their sins by taking the life of their later children. It is a lonely, fearful road to travel.

But I have Good News for those women! The Bible says:

If we confess our sins, he is faithful and just to forgive
us our sins, and to cleanse us from all unrighteousness.

1 John 1:9

That includes abortion! Jesus died on the Cross for every sin of every kind. He didn't put stipulations on which sins were forgivable. Yes, The Ten Commandments say, "Thou shalt not kill." But they also say not to commit adultery, be jealous of other's possessions, lie on people, or disrespect your parents. In God's eyes, they are all sin, and they are all forgivable. If you can believe John 3:16, you can believe Hebrews 10:16-17:

This is the covenant that I will make with them after
those days, saith the Lord, I will put my laws into their
hearts, and in their minds will I write them; And
their sins and iniquities will I remember no more.

The Psalms tell us:

He hath not dealt with us after our sins; nor rewarded
us according to our iniquities. For as the heaven is high
above the earth, so great is his mercy toward them that
fear him. As far as the east is from the west, so far hath he
removed our transgressions from us. Like as a father pitieth
his children, so the Lord pitieth them that fear him.

Psalm 103:10-13

God is not out to seek retribution for abortion. He is a loving Father who knows everything about the decision to abort that child. He knows the circumstances, the stress, the pressure other people exerted, the immaturity of the woman in some cases, the humiliation of pregnancy because of how it occurred, and every other variable that went into the decision. We are human – we make mistakes – we sin. God knows that and doesn't hold it against Christian women. Sounds strange that

Christian women have abortions, but statistics show that about 20% of all abortions are conducted for women who profess Christianity. For those women, it is even harder to stop self-condemnation because they knew better but did it anyway. God still forgives. He also has a way of using negative circumstances and choices and turning them into powerful testimonies for the Kingdom.

And we know that all things work together
for good to them that love God, to them who
are the called according to his purpose.
Romans 8:28

Women who have had abortions often have nightmares that last for years, and many encounter problems in relationships because of the secret guilt and shame they carry. The scar of abortion also holds regret: for the actions that led to the pregnancy, for the abortion, for the secrecy and shame, and for not raising the child.

If you are one of those women, turn it over to God. Confess your sin, ask His forgiveness, and leave the sin at the Cross. Don't pick it back up. Your unborn child is with God in heaven, and if you have accepted Jesus Christ as your Lord and Savior, you will meet and spend eternity loving that child. All aborted children are in God's merciful hands forever. None of them will ever be in hell; they will always be with God throughout eternity. God forgives you unconditionally. Your salvation is intact. God is not going to hit you with a brick or strike you with lightning. His mercies are new every morning. God's Word says you are forgiven. Now you must forgive yourself. If you don't, you are telling God that Jesus' sacrifice on the Cross for your sins was not sufficient, that His shed blood wasn't enough to cover your sins, and that you know better than God (which, of course, you don't!).

I acknowledge my sin unto thee, and mine iniquity have
I not hid. I said, I will confess my transgressions unto the
Lord; and thou forgavest the iniquity of my sin. Selah.
Psalm 32:5

PRAYER FOR ABORTION/ FORGIVENESS

Hear the cry of each woman and man who mourns the loss of their child to abortion. Forgive my sins, restore me to Your grace and calm my spirit. I release sorrow to You and ask You to fill the void in my heart with Your generous love.

I denounce the stronghold of the enemy and claim freedom from attempts to keep me bound. Help me to realize and accept that Jesus paid the price, so I am free. Help me dear Lord, to stand fast in the liberty by which Christ has made me free. Remind me that I am redeemed.

I pray that I am released from the bondage of shame, and now replaced with God's refreshing love and peace. Today, let the Balm of Gilead soothe my soul in our loving Jesus name, Amen.

If we confess our sins, he is faithful and just to forgive us our sins, and to cleanse us from all unrighteousness.

I John 1:9

CHAPTER 14

DANCING WITH THE SCARS

Peace I leave with you, my peace I give unto you:
not as the world giveth, give I unto you.
Let not your heart be troubled, neither let it be afraid.

John 14:27

Most of us have heard of the popular TV series that started in 2005 called *Dancing with the Stars*. It used to be one of my favorite shows. I enjoyed the moving and grooving, and the high energy dancing, flipping and flopping, and vacillating back and forth. The show was full of excitement! Now dancing itself is a time of celebrating, whether you are at a wedding, a party, or rejoicing in church. Dancing is an expression of joy.

While I understand people dancing with partners at a club, a wedding party, school dance, prom, or other special celebrations, dancing with scars is a little different type of dance. This dance is designed to encourage people who have fallen, but who got back up and refused to quit. There is life after your loss; there is life after divorce; there is life after failure. You do not stop - you keep moving forward.

Because we are alive, we get hurt. We have wounds. Those wounds eventually heal, and often leave scars. Scars are not open wounds; they are wounds that have healed. They are our testimonies of the journeys we have taken, the experiences we have had, and the lessons we have learned. They are not to be hidden under a bushel. We can use our scars to shed light on healing for others suffering from the same kinds of wounds. People tend to hide their scars, but Jesus did not hide His scars. He wasn't ashamed of His scars. They proclaimed the road He had traveled and the tough journey He had endured. They showed the trials that God brought Him through.

The Bible says Jesus was, "marred more than any man" (Isaiah 52:14). If Jesus was not immune, and we are to be like Him, then we should expect to carry some scars.

Scars show us where we have been,
they do not dictate where we are going.

–David Rossi

God is in the healing business. He heals our wounds. He heals our brokenness, our emotional pain, the guilt of our past sins, and the hurt that other people have inflicted on us. Those invisible wounds can be deep, permanent, intentional, or accidental. Wounds come from many physical and emotional causes, but they all leave scars. Once the scar tissue forms, we are careful to avoid getting wounded again. We protect ourselves and try to keep the scar from reopening and waking up the pain inside.

Instead, what if we decided to make peace with our scars? Decided to feel blessed that God carried us through our wounds and pain, and we made it safely to healing? Decided that we don't have to protect ourselves from future scars but instead choose to live our lives in freedom? Physicians can treat physical scar tissue to make it less noticeable. The scar is still there, but you pay less attention to it. God can do the same with emotional scars. He is the Great Physician. The scar may still be there, but God can take away the pain and replace it with joy and peace that passes all understanding.

He healeth the broken in heart,
and bindeth up their wounds.

Psalm 147:3

We all carry scars of some sort, some more egregious than others. How we carry them is our choice. We can live with pain and heartache and let our scars cause bitterness and bring out ugliness and hurt, or we can choose to move past it and find our joy in life again. We can learn to dance with our scars. We can choose not to give up, not to be in despair, and not to quit. Dancing connotates pleasure, joy, happiness, and celebration. We can be set free and be liberated from our wounds. We can see our scars as battle trophies for the challenges we overcame. Here is what the Bible says about it:

And he said unto me, My grace is sufficient for thee: for my strength is made perfect in weakness. Most gladly therefore will I rather glory in my infirmities, that the power of Christ may rest upon me. Therefore I take pleasure in infirmities, in reproaches, in necessities, in persecutions, in distresses for Christ's sake: for when I am weak, then am I strong.
2 Corinthians 12:9-10

Scar tissue is different from normal skin but is evidence of God's power to heal you and change you.

For I will restore health unto thee, and I will heal thee of thy wounds, saith the Lord; because they called thee an Outcast, saying, This is Zion, whom no man seeketh after.
Jeremiah 30:17

All you have to do to get a touch from God is to call out to Him. He will hear your cry.

Then they cry unto the Lord in their trouble, and he saveth them out of their distresses. He sent his word, and healed them, and delivered them from their destructions.
Psalm 107:19-20

Jeremiah tells us:

Heal me, O Lord, and I shall be healed; save me,
and I shall be saved: for thou art my praise.
Jeremiah 17:14

When you choose healing and joy, remember to thank God for restoring you to wholeness. He can remove the hurt, fill the void, and give meaning to your life again.

Blessed be God, even the Father of our Lord Jesus Christ,
the Father of mercies, and the God of all comfort;
Who comforteth us in all our tribulation, that we may
be able to comfort them which are in any trouble, by the
comfort wherewith we ourselves are comforted of God.
2 Corinthians 1:3-4

And remember, above all, God wants you to prosper, to be in health, and to have life abundantly.

Beloved, I wish above all things that thou mayest
prosper and be in health, even as thy soul prospereth.
3 John 2

Choose life, choose happiness, and dance often in celebration of and with your scars. God will use them and you to bring glory to the Kingdom. Don't let your scars discourage or disappoint you. It doesn't matter what scars you are dealing with:

- Loneliness
- Losing a loved one
- Humiliation
- Shame and guilt
- Betrayal
- Rape and molestation

- Offense and unforgiveness
- Regret
- Addiction
- Suicide
- Abortion

It is time for restoration! Dance with your scars! God is turning your scars into stars, just as He did with Jesus' scars. After Christ died on the Cross, He was only known by His scars, people didn't recognize Him until they saw His nail-scarred hands. God used Jesus' sacrifice to save all men from their sins. Don't you know that Jesus danced with joy once the suffering was finished! You can be like Jesus: Dance with your scars into your future with celebration and hope.

For I know the plans I have for you," declares the Lord,
"plans to prosper you and not to harm you,
plans to give you hope and a future.
Jeremiah 29:11 (NIV)

REFERENCES

Holt-Lunstad, J., Smith, T.B., & Layton, J.B. (2010). Social relationships and mortality risk: a meta-analytic review. PLoS Medicine, 7(7), e1000316. doi:10.1371/journal.pmed.1000316.

Risk factors and warning signs. (2020, January 24). Retrieved May 13, 2020, from https://afsp.org/risk-factors-and-warning-signs

Ross, E. K. (1973). *On death and dying.* London: Tavistock Pubs.

Shaw, M. E. (2008). *The heart of addiction: a biblical perspective.* Bemidji, MN: Focus.

Ware, B. (2019). *The top five regrets of the dying: a life transformed by the dearly departing.* Alexandria, NSW: Hay House Australia.

Webb, R. (2015). *Destroying the Root of Racism.* Rolla, MO: Chalfant Eckert Publishing.

CPSIA information can be obtained
at www.ICGtesting.com
Printed in the USA
LVHW052159010721
691613LV00005B/9